A Place in the World

IAIN BAMFORTH has lived with his wife and two children in Strasburg since 1995. In addition to his three books of poetry with Carcanet, Verso publish his literary history of medicine, *The Body in the Library*, and his collection of essays on medicine and modernity. In a varied career, he has been general practitioner, outback doctor, lecturer, translator and literary journalist.

Also by Iain Bamforth from Carcanet

Sons and Pioneers
Open Workings

IAIN BAMFORTH

A Place in the World

Poems 1996–2002

So he stood in his shoes
And he wondered,
He wondered,
He stood in his
Shoes and he wondered.
John Keats

CARCANET

Acknowledgements

To the editors of the following: *Verse*, *Metre*, *TLS*, *Quadrant* (Australia), *Parnassus* (USA), *La Revue Commune* (France), *British Journal of General Practice*, *PN Review*, *The Scotsman*, *Southfields*, *Poetry Review*, *The Red Wheelbarrow*. 'A Nest of Boxes' was first published in Alec Finlay's *Without Day: Proposals for a New Scottish Parliament* (Pocketbooks, 2000).

First published in Great Britain in 2005 by
Carcanet Press Limited
Alliance House
Cross Street
Manchester M2 7AQ

A CIP catalogue record for this book is available from the British Library
ISBN 1 85754 760 8

The publisher acknowledges financial assistance from Arts Council England

Typeset in Monotype Ehrhardt by XL Publishing Services, Tiverton
Printed and bound in England by SRP Ltd, Exeter

Contents

Third-Person Lion

Be the lion, fired by brightness,
the third-person lion
trained by the wakened mind
to defy all churchmen foes,
the vindictive godly ones
with connections in the town.

(Pharisees who want the lion tagged.)

The lion roared, in consciousness
of the German language
at the bars of which no lion is brief.
For in Göttingen, as in Greece,
the man who owns a lion
is owned by the lion too.

(Diogenes of Sinope, who said it first.)

Needy, needier than ever perhaps,
I begged my gibbous master
for the secret of his science,
the freedom of a human reading.
Philosophy, he said with a grin,
is modern lion management.

(One of our many service industries.)

A splendid beast, that lion
out of Hogarth read by Lichtenberg.
Here it stands, thistlefine,
emblazoned in a mane of light.
Its distinctive sin is pride.
This be its written constitution.

A Charm for Europe

For the bestiary without a name,
for great wet bladders sagging in the rain,
for the thing you have to push-start
(methane-machine with twelve apostles on her flank),
for the plastic-wrap triplicate wayslip,
for unbothered gaffers at the selection ramp,
for the way disgust gets up your nose
and every slithery, slipped-on stumbling block,
for those who've never cherished the word *boustrophedon*
or heard a fly-descant musing at their shoulder
or stopped to sing, in a field of clover,
the song of vachardise, the song of vachardise,
for those who keep insisting to anyone who'll listen
let me out please I'm a British ruminant;

for the grandees of The Pied Cow,
for haulers of goods across the asphalt pastures
(dumb flayed divinity of the ledger books),
for those with their heads down, those snug in the skin
of the ancient flea-ridden pantomime pin-tail,
for flesh-eaters choking on the fricasee of their want,
for those who'd gag the Chagall cow,
for hand foot and mouth doctors with a bone to pick,
for the brazen revolutionary heifer pissing at the wind,
for the ventripotent, the chagrin-mongers,
for those milking cows they can,
and for every lurking disease that might be
in the constitution of Europe
and adhering to cellulose.

Tobias Smollett in the Var

Having survived various *aubergistes*
and the chanter of the laddie-weans,
the Dignity of Physick came, in person,
to Fréjus, with its amphitheatre
and the distant prospect of Esterelles –
high point on the road to Italy –
and shivered silly in the post-house:
snow on the pines at the back
(that he might think himself in Scotland)
but frontward, looking south,
sun-dappled juniper, box and lavender,
a most singular vista of the sea,
and the scented tree, in reach of the window,
exhaling its zest of oranges.
Rigour *and* bounty! Beyond was Cannes,
a little fishing town.

Rough Sleeper

Making their still warm bed this morning
Robinson couldn't help but notice the snarled fissure
up the middle of his side,
furrowed, tectonic, divided against itself;
a suture that refuses to fuse
on the bark of its sameness, mark
of his journeys downwards
to what is neither salt nor fresh nor entirely
living thing, where squames of light
fall in some untroubled blue.

Imagine: he pushed the boat out last night –
swimming for hours and hours
towards land, or what he remembers as land,
but was perhaps a Sargasso
creased by wind, some brooding moonlit stretch
forced to raging by his aimlessness
and tilting one way or the other
under its dome of vastness, bereft of her.
A place in sleep so deep
it crumples like a canvas sail.

Being tired is something delicate,
somewhere high and dry. After hours of graft
he might yield to it, the sweet solicitation
that lapses him, labouring
for the possible wakening, the one will
of his bluntly mutineering body.
Nothing on that horizon can be a help to Robinson
now he's made the bed for today,
packing his thunder sail
beneath those strict ribs sunk into the shore.

Disgruntlements

To hell with humankind!
It's enough to make you give up doctoring!
I keep telling myself this
is the last time I ever want to see anyone –
after all, what's it to me
if they want to outdo the Joneses, deep-freeze the Golden Calf,
    or look serene on St John's Wort?
Though I hardly have to catch sight of a face
and I love it again.

(Goethe)

Got a lot? Expect quite soon
to own a whole lot more.
Don't have much? You'd better learn
what asset-stripping means.

And if you don't possess a jot –
sot, best start digging:
the right to live is
had by those who have.

(Heine)

Voyage au Pays du Fer

for John Western

1

Not forsaken, not one, the unemployed
assembling at the pithead, another
using another kind of carbon to note down
the message leaking from the future.

2

One or two guard their own lights
talking intently in the cold, tense-lunged.

Prisoners who've staked their freedom,
canaries in the mineshaft
that runs under France and Germany.

The spinning of the earth gives way
to the hollow of their hands
and a zodiac mountain in two minds.

3

They go walking underneath the Flood
to Louis Agassiz's glacial slicks.

To the tar pits set aside
for the miner as a man in history.

4

I wonder at them, pretending
to be so literal-minded,
the red bus home to a damp bed,
supper, television, and the vertical dreams
of an era, massacred at the rock face.
Ariadne, with her thread.

5

It was their grandparents
first planted these sunflowers
in their gardens, Polish
children from northern Europe
stumbling over terse
phrases for neighbourhoods
packed and curled like ammonite.

6

Couples sauntered
through the woods of wild garlic

then slept together
like whales, head down:

a nasal unison
droning through their heads,

not worry was it
just Sisyphus on their hands.

7

Underground, I've been told,
is out of bounds now,

foreknowledge
breached and harrowed,

thick grass fat
at the glacier's heel.

8

Foreknowledge of what?

Every day the boulder clay's
inexhaustible capital of flesh and fauna
threatens to erode.

By documentary marvel
I can dream them
labouring on beneath the viaducts
to where a rock
is cleaved of understanding
and a train groans
moving its millennial mass.

10

Some of them must have spent half a life
on rock mattresses, stretched out
to undermine even that upholstering.

It all vanishes in the rain.
They dug for something swollen in their words,
though often they didn't speak at all.

11

Historians settle
for what they find, the known thing
torn from a list of mercantile
instances, quenched
arrears on that heroic discomfort
held like a trophy aloft
till a slow wave comes.

12

How else to claim the edge
in a world submerged by endeavour
slackening into stories,

yellow poisonous air
killing the precious thing with wings
for miles around?

Pascal –
his eyes almost gone,
his joints almost stone themselves

tells me he came back to the black
after the last war,
gouged out a few desultory knots:

keepsakes
for his children's children
to one day lay bare.

Diggers, luggers, placemarkers:

they stepped out once
in a bright spill of light
and something altogether blown
quickened in their hands.

Who's crying havoc?
It's only pain, unmeaning
everything. Not
as grand as Piranesi's
architecture, or an escaped
fire-dragon.

No archaeology either.
It's only as deep
as the skin across the world,
bitter cold air
lunging at you, a razor
over stubble ground.

No brilliant explosion,
though it brought you, lone
figure at the face,
under a weight of stone,
a sense of what goes wrong,
keeps faith and shuffles home.

16

Put it like this, he said,
it was more a matter of reaching up
than being dragged down.

Metzange, Lorraine

Strasburg Event

Hold a conversation (Prospero to Ariel) in which everything refers to Europe.

When someone calls down the stars of the twelve apostles suggest things are more like they are now than they've ever been.

When someone talks about universal rights, extending you an equal portion of Ariadne's string, take her to one of Shakespeare's knot-gardens.

When someone mentions rising expectations ask where Europe's working class assembles now: in the chalk circles of Caucasia?

And when someone extols the wealth of nations remember Vallejo's hunger for the Word.

If you've nothing to say in the deserts of Bohemia – friend, adversary, prosecutor – say it in your own language.

Quatrain

François Villon

My name is France's – one of the scum;
From Paris (near Pontoise) I come.
Soon from my neck will pend the sum
Of a torso plus a bum.

Calvin's Architect

He loathed arches, 'which were never at rest',
and put them inside, as a provocation, where nobody would see them.
John Bull got rounder by the day,
but he preferred straight lines, the mind led away
at an angle, distraught into the infinite.
He rebuilt an undertaker's Egypt in the middle of Glasgow,
warehouses from Nineveh, terraces from Athens:
the Vast, the Magnificent, the Terrible, the Brilliant, the Obscure.
One should never be a slave to style or dead forms –
for architecture was a log of human enterprise
handed on from the councils of eternity,
'imperishable thoughts', in friable Giffnock sandstone;
great voids of glass in their iron coffins.

Despairing of the nineteenth century's lack
of architectural distinction, he made it manly and sublime,
at least the loudly denigrated parts of it
that stood for rectitude above the furnaces, the waste dumps, the ash–cries
out of Dante:
architecture, not to endure time
but to show us how eschatology saves us from time
in Presbyterian temples, Solomonic attics.
All his plans measured in cubits.

The Window

Rilke in Paris

He dreamt he pushed his life along
the street, and climbed the stairs of Sacré Coeur
stealing a march on hunger pangs;
his own, and those of poor
folk tugging on his coat. He visited Rodin
who cut amused into a slab
of righteousness, and called it man.
The dream said Paris was a honeycomb.

He climbed into his rented
space, three up, inviting hammer blows
to punch him in the mouth, pent
language riot in a maze
of bellowing. Hôtel-Dieu was full of men
like him, soft heads, hard ribs;
the dream sucked through a vortex of ambition.
Now the longing seemed drab;

the fog of faces Byzantine. He crawled
into his bunk. Steps
thickened, then the dream. A crowd
poured up the stairs. Perhaps
he'd open – Not now, not as long
as the street reeked iodine
and animal fat. Bleating
green arithmetic, Paris drove over him.

Baudelaire: Albatross

Often, to kill time, the men on board
will snare that huge sea-bird, the albatross.
It hangs astern as if our boat soared
like a water-walker on the abyss.

Hardly bundled on deck, this hamstrung king
flaps and flounders in a rush of pride,
helpless as each huge white wing
flails, a clackety oar, at his side.

No cloud-rider he, so clumsy and weak!
Monarch of the air? Must be Colonel Blimp.
Some sailor sticks a roll-up in his beak;
another apes his spastic limp.

Genus *poet*, playboy of the higher spheres,
he glides over weathers, out of aim;
but now he's grounded jeers
call him freak whose wingspan lames him.

Questions for Chekhov

You were no man for evangelical discomfort,
no ascetic of the Sermon on the Mount:
so what drove you to the limit, yours and Russia's,
and made you, briefly, prison inspector?

The carriage that took you was unspringed.
Novosibirsk, Yenisey, Baikal, Amur:
dry feet (you noticed) were the highest good;
distance in the taiga lived on and on.

Opening the door directly on the Milky Way
you surprised yourself, recognising
desolation's deepest ore in a convict's speech.
(Better said: your body recognised it, craving sleep.)

Was that what it took to be inspector
of the bare-faced? The only voices in the island
seemed the wind's. Eskimo wisdom
out of Diogenes: vastness far from human.

Diogenes Looking for Humans

When anyone asked him where he came from, he said, 'I am a citizen of the world.'
Diogenes Laertius, *Life of Diogenes the Cynic*

1

Reason, Diogenes saw, was homeless in the cities:
all the more to be a pedestrian advocate
of ascetic happiness, to live not needing things.

Athenians, he saw, were stiff with virtue
(being seen to be virtuous) when what made them moral
was the lurid publicising of the inner life –
always running after things they already had!

Bounty and postponement, their parables of agape:
living in the supermarket and not the city!

2

In search of the deeper truth of humans living together
Diogenes moved with his personal effects
to a dog-house at the city gate.

He called it Plato's Cave.
Plato called him Socrates gone mad.
He had stamped on pride, but only with another pride.

3

Theory and praxis –
Diogenes picked them clean
in case he met a human
and felt like biting him.
This, he said, was the only
lesson of philanthropy.
Being his doctrine's medium
he lived what he said;
said what he lived –
affront and effrontery:
the plebeian street philosophy.

4

Diogenes' mottos:

The wise man enjoys all things
but only if he can do quite as well without.

The wise man may be a fool
but not the fool of his own needs.

5

The cosmic citizen was troubled. His lesson was simple.
Yet he doubted whether it would be understood
now people lived in comfortable estrangement.

What they called cynicism was something integrated –
knowing how the world is, doing nothing about it;

their hard-baked realism the global circumstance
of the old ideals, in modern hygienic forms.

Diogenes – renouncing one identity to save another!

6

Shortly before his arrest
for disorderly conduct
and offences against public morals
he took the name *Jesus* –
impertinent sovereignty
loosed into society.

A Vision

Beyond the window, on a cold and empty
morning at the Hôtel de Ville,
a host of chiliastic guillotines stand
before the Nation's altar
and exercise their right to silence
each critic of the constitution
(the guillotine: a doctor's
invention just like Roget's catacomb
for the language of the globe –
one of Reason's steel-cold instruments
for ridding heads of ballast)
when, beneath one of the tumbrels,
and to the great involuntary surprise
of the cat-calling multitude
Panurge heaves into view, whistling
while he stitches heads back onto necks,
in this case, brave Epistemon's,
wryneck to the court of King Anarch –

(though his heart, it seems, had melted
before his limbs were broken
and the dogs had already undone
compassion's very bowels –
like washing snatched from the line
in a skit by Aesop out of La Fontaine).

Gauguin: Self-Portrait near Golgotha

Time swaddles the House of Pleasure.
Days beneath a canopy
of pandanus leaves, in the tourist season,
he grasps what it means: scandal.
Stumbles over it himself. On the floor
rosewood carvings planted long ago
like doubts (self-justifying ones), announce
with squat omniscience
the flourishing of Vincent's ear.
Tohutaua has – long since – left his bed
and gone back to her husband's.
Citrus spells green. Hibiscus red.
In the half-light he smells them, seeing neither.
Far off, he watches stout neighbours
carrying an old man (an ancestor?)
to the water's edge, and laving him
He stands on the edge of sleep
(slips into it the way the stars unhinge
and tumble into the Pacific, carnal
flowers in some divine stock exchange.)
He fingers the wound again,
the native hardwood sweaty with the darg.
For he recognises the place, Golgotha
in Polynesia, overripe colours
that have nothing to do with threadbare
patience, the distant Breton view
of low clouds and stunted trees,
fields unfenced to the coming night.
He asks for it to pass from him – not to be
a man of sorrows nailed to his culture.

Glosses

LICHTENBERG'S REPLIQUE
The louder they proclaim themselves free
the more obviously they're prisoners,
at least of their references.

*

CHITTERLINGS
I asked for Rabelais, and got Pascal's
angel-beasts, tormented by music –
the squeakings, gibberings and honkings
of a monstrous Tabernacle Choir.

*

A CARGO CULT
They introduced the rights of man
and I beheld the wondrous sight:
a massive levelling, envy among neighbours.

*

DIDEROT
Those Frenchmen pen a thistle-sharp Encyclopaedia
but hate mention of Rameau's ghastly nephew.

*

BEYOND SUSPICION
Spinoza's beatitude –
the certainty of having been eternal.

*

VOICE-BOX
The larynx: the body's revenge on the mind.

*

READING LEIBNIZ
The mildest sea of meaning
makes a hollow sound
now drains have been installed
in the Kingdom of Entelechy.

*

RUMPELSTILTZCHEN
Nobody has guessed the bad-tempered dwarf's
proper name is 'wrinkled foreskin' –
but soon everyone will know, even the princess.

*

THE JACOBIN CLUB
Whatever they do is done with the best of intentions.
So they go, forgiving themselves in advance.

*

SADE
Staring from his Paris prison window
at the hundred guillotines of Pure Reason
he calls for a manicure.

*

MORE ON ANGELS
That fractional silence between TV programmes
is an angel crossing the room. In Russia
the same embarrassment
is attributed to a policeman being born.

*

GANYMEDE
A realist who hadn't made his mind up
about reality...
           Sad to say reality
made its mind up about him.

*

A FUTUROLOGIST
With bad grace, quite against his will,
he registers a fossil track –
otherwise he wouldn't know which
Long Ago is a Not Yet.

*

LOVE IN THE WESTERN WORLD
If desire were wise
it wouldn't be desire –
engagement and flight,
the exact self-fit
of a stumbling block.

*

IMPÔTS
Admire France's
tactless body politic –

every citizen autopsied
by a tax inspector,

even the visiting poet
obliged to surrender

his poems to the language
as 'tender taxes'.

CREDO
If I'm a believer?
                    – God only knows.

Tongues and Claws

Arp, who smeared the blessed meaningless word
with the musk of pure forgiveness
when fathers started turning their sons into trees
without a fig, and not even a leaf;

Arp, dada juggler of the Trinity:
on one side of the border he was Hans,
on the other plain old Jean,
until they came together, under a wooden star;

Arp, his tongue thick with snails
and an ink-stained zodiac of absurd intentions,
imperial elephants with worn-out teeth,
storks, frogs, assorted royalty,
and other cherubim harnessed to the Alps.

Was isch? he grins, and cuts your throat with a fork.

Eggs called Chaos

I look at these stones and know little about them,
But I know their gates are open too,
Always open, far longer open, than any bird's can be...
                                        Hugh MacDiarmid

On the other side of the globe
walking where the day
begins, I leaned against the wind
and under a sun-warped Samoan adobe
listened to that soft roar
when the swell turns back, stunned
to be on a beach that was molten glass.
Then I noticed the door

opening in a stone, and I swore

I was back in Scotland,
getting real, pushed out to the edge of my life
by the curved beach at Whalsay
and the grain of sand
that had escaped a landscape harder than bone.
I cradled it, weighed it in my palm,
a gloss on what can't be
buried, one of the language-stones

drawn from a cairn of groans:

such eyeless potatoes
as might sprout flowers
or announce catastrophe in time for tea.
No, nothing grows
from quinsies like theirs, so unlike
a pomegranate or the geode in my mother's knee,
simple minds that say
'throw' or 'strike'

and shoulder to shoulder form a dyke

against the tarry sea of sin.
Core is all they are,
so like itself there's nothing else to feel
but chill sobriety against the skin.
I can't think of less
than those riddled Quaternary mountains
still under compulsion
for imitating consciousness,

moving out of wetness

and cast, like insults, on the shore.
Lichenified or salt-scrubbed,
they dazzle me from behind the Flood;
more energy in every pore
than a mass of light
expelled to a universe of levity.
Eggs called Chaos. I know their slob language
and want to fight

giant stirrings in the night

like some peasant on a medieval ergot high;
but you, thrower, try to be a cold
evangelist of discomfort;
and will be, by God, if you cry
in the middle of the night, and wait –
querulous Irish saint –
for the return of the flat-stone coracle,
for the Scottish state

that needs a hard man at the gate

to separate the sheep
from the granite-clambering goats.
Stones are pregnant only
with their own meaning, not deep
but enough to fill a pocket,
good for sucking on
as a cure for stammerers,
a growling nacreous bucket

that would love to make a racket

if only let loose
upon an unsuspecting world.
I listened to that sublime dark roar,
not needing an excuse
to be halfway round
the globe's blunt core, on the beach at Falesa,
and let myself in, closing the door
on the partly drowned,

on the lives of stones, and what I found.

The Stone Toad

Well, it happened to one of the labouring men, in breaking the stones to make metal for the new road, that he broke a stone that was both large and remarkable, and in the heart of it, which was boss, there was found a living creature, that jumped out the moment it saw the light of heaven, to the great terrification of the man, who could think it was nothing but an evil spirit that has been imprisoned there in a time... But when we came to the spot, it was just a yird toad, and the laddie weans nevelled it to death with stones, before I could persuade them to give over.

John Galt, *Annals of the Parish*, Chapter 10

Galt in his *Annals of the Parish*
– a bestseller in 1821
before he'd gridplanned south Ontario –
mentions a slab of matter
found when building the Ayr road.
It was jemmied open,
coconut-wise, for the primal sound
of Scotland as the universe.

Bossed inside was a petrifaction,
a moral third dimension
that wasn't inert, because it blinked.
Once. Poor fat bourgeois toad,
before it could even karaoke *Figaro!*
stoned – by half of Ayr.
Stoned so thoroughly it was heavier
than the letter of the law.

Live irony brained by deep time!
It made me wonder at
our heresy (let mind be other) –
how pandemonium could stay alive
in a schist of caledon
or a toad's head form the thought
enlightened by a fatal
id of lost reality...

Stone, you are a stumbling block
I told myself, recalling
Galt and the serpentine out of Ayr,
an old yird toad peeling
too late the membrane from its eye –
Lot's wife, in reverse...
Ours is consciousness after;
a wink not being what one thinks.

Coal Fish

Ventilation in the earlier part of last century was a negligible quantity, and the air was often too foul for the naked-light lamps to burn in. One old man told me that he remembered some sixty years ago working below ground by the phosphorescent light of decaying fish-heads, in a low part of the mine where the air was too foul to allow his tallow lamp to burn. He said they gave him enough light to show him where to 'howk' his coal.

David Rorie, *The Mining Folk of Fife*, 1914

Go back, swimmer in your swimming life,
to the estuary's mareel of light
shelved by the bed, to a coal-black night
omenless, lambent with the strife

it takes to live a hero's life
aboard a raft of excruciating faces –
ruffed sequinned spaces
cleft by their landing on the knife.

Fish. They visit you from dire straits, life-
forms unfathomed in the air:
coldly trembling, seething on the stair
to their deep-sea trench. Rife

in a glitter, they slide through life
– each strung reprieve – till all you know
of what frets them is a slow
flood of light in the mines of Fife.

They burn about you on the Tree of Life;
integer, relic a fish called coal,
industrious rapt soul
of how it is. Light of a life.

Gideon's Bible in a Late Night Motel

Let me embarrass you with a prophecy
(let me first embarrass myself)
of the world transfigured:
no flickering thought more candid
than the bedroom
scathed with snow, its weak
propitiousness and matrimonial vows
confused by the massive bulk
of a century, lapsing.

An ordinary scene from the early years
of our post-literate future,
His response: supply-side. Hers –
upping everything, even the *ante*:
gone to California
the year of Level Above Human,
the pixilated gender wars,
Jesus of Utah coming to a mall near everyone.
All-Nite floats on Chaos.

Europa and the Whale

EUROPA
We make so many things of you –
cranks, pedals, horns, the pulley belt.
You're a large Atlantic hill
vacuuming the people back to bones
the ancient squabble of the flesh.

WHALE
Go find your pitch pot, cosmopolitan –
don't you remember the rank smell
of your Venice of achievement,
the cellar looted and the library on fire,
Captain Nemo's underwater arias?

EUROPA
We so admire your tuba and euphonium
concerto for the century roar
of Mr Ives (or was it Mr Deeds?)
but don't expect to get Huzzahs!
when your art of music goes to war.

*

Boot of the Big Dipper.
Grand hooded phantom.
Sandhill of Nantucket.
Noah Webster's ark.

In its belly-slime
so many Shakers
murmur for the spirit
of the shaker God.

*

EUROPA
America of the happy-shiny,
appointed people of the Golden Age –
isn't there another way to seek the Lord
in your high vault of a Wurlitzer?

We object to your cold hysteria.
your pitch and blubber freight,
your feeling for the plummetless.
So tuck your guts back in.

Where do you think you are –
letting it all hang loose
like Jonah on the *Oprah!* show.
(Little baleen's watching too…)

*

*A whale goes many
days into the deep.
The low sun fades
on Nineveh.*

*Memory and act:
the forms change
but the crisis
stays the same.*

The Wound Man

after a line drawing by Gersdorf, Feldtbuch des Wundartzney, *Strasburg, 1530*

'Toubib,
            I hardly recognised you today
handing out your visiting card as the wound man.
Is this what you mean by trial and error,
feeling how the hurt-words cut,
bare as need yourself?'
                        'It's all I *can* mean
trying to keep my sympathy intact.
I thought I understood the social contract. Now
it seems we're administered by dogmatists,
virtue accountants, moral Esperantists.
Do you think I cared for the unfortunate
for what I got out of them?'
                                'How much then?'
'Less than you'd imagine. I can't even make
ends meet…'
                'But wise up, man –
no doctor ever abandoned his livelihood
to become a shaman, undefiled by money!'

'Once it *was* too sacred to be paid –'

'What does that mean? That you've lived
harder, deeper than us all, maimed
by the pristine man you thought you were?
Taking the money keeps you humble!
And now you've lost your reason,
become carnage to the job!'
                                'Soul needed saving
and I never insisted on the money anyway.
Whose reason do you mean anyway?'

'But it's the providential state that pays you!
Too many doctors I suppose,
and you dispensing hope, not eternal life!'

'I couldn't sell what the French consider hope.
It was mortification, a most abject kind.'

'Isn't it remarkable the way a doctor asserts
authority even as he yields it up!
Wasn't "heal yourself Herr Arzt" inscribed
on those dog-eared poetry journals
in your waiting room?'
                              'I try to live
my own restraint, the Scottish way with intellect.
It took me years to discover charity,
to be put out by the rain in other people's heads
or shiver at a face beneath the ice.
But that *is* charity – negating what you value most:
your self.'
                    'You mean: you didn't have the stamina
to play the vanity game, or turn on the charm?
No wonder every distraction was a disaster.'

'I hoped for wisdom as an epic form of truth
and understanding as a reciprocity.
Nothing prepared me for the lack of affability;
indifference as the root of tolerance:
the wound left gaping: unrepaired by
tact. Hence my distress at our utopia of blind
archaic fears and childish wants:
body, since its layers are only envelope,
can never become knowledge.
That is the heresy of the end of days.'

'Go then, see if you can find insouciance.'

The House-Boat

My friend in the deep north tells me of an old man
on Foula, that sub-Arctic dependency,
who was known to go out, winter or summer,
to flay himself a tractable skin of peat.

When asked, he said: *This is an old fire;*
it has never gone out in my lifetime
of cutting and trimming and slow burning.

What he forgot to mention, living under it himself,
was the other use of turf: as a rig
self-sealed against the weather's plans in mind.

When he died, in the iron compass of his talk,
his neighbours smoored the sempiternal
source of warmth. Months later
a roof was seen indolently careening seawards

In the Republic of Virtue

Two birds go frantic
in our Adam and Eve pear-tree,
tiny mechanical sirens
of the Fifth – weren't the others good enough? – Republic.

One needles the other:
'We must wipe all impurity from the face of
France.' And the retort –
'Pray uninterruptedly, brother!'

The dandy that holds the line
is Rameau's nephew,
the plain one a citizen of Geneva;
and both are orators in our garden by the Rhine.

Pig Melon Incarnation

1

Sour little melons of the bush,
only good for being spat out,
so bitter-aloes on the tongue;
yet months later you've overrun
the vineyards of Engedi –

in that hot austral December
of Leonids and Geminids
string on string of
meteor-showers wriggled up
out of attraction's basin,

hundreds of tiny surveillance
pods with a purchase on the planet.
Landmines of endolymph,
yours are the laws of air
that quilt this vacant ground.

2

Here, there's no visible water;
only its smell, if you've a nose
for such an anxious thing:
double hydrogen humming
for oxygen's slug gills.

I watch you siphon a crust of
salt, each inquisitorial
taproot sucking moisture
from the hyperbolic future.
Soil-burrowers, tongues

in search of righteousness
wandering miles into aridity
(though righteousness, I have
to remark, isn't really
what I came to find).

3

What then? Only to stand
in huge red indifference
not knowing the rules, and watch
you, organic dirigibles,
get ready for a maiden flight?

Little melons, you need no liquid
bed, no preparation
for the coming day, tongues
at earth level, rough
and moist and deeply colluding.

Time is your little word of moan,
rind of a speech-bubble
begging for light, inwardness,
stages of recognition
when the flesh is at a distance.

4

Sour little melons of the bush,
I'm still gathering you –
Solomon's exaggerations
from my childhood with the Lord.
Your hair is what I fly on.

I'll say nothing of the burning bush
or your anemophilic
pollen, giant night undressing
what is spanned by air,
or my own attempts to be a river.

In short, no desert miracle
thinking I'd seen a melon incarnation.
These are its sheddings,
soft flakes of light
newly outcast from the air.

Cares of a Family Man

In our living room a creature
coaxes a language free of its muzzle.
Sometimes it clicks and stutters,
or makes long-drawn-out
breath sounds, the plaintive *krâ-krâ*
of a Kalahari bushman.

Its name is something choked
– Odradek (says K). 'It lurks by turns
in the garret, the stairway, the lobby, the hall.'
Not to ask, not to be answered –
hospitality is suddenly
stricken, and dogs us like grief.

Well and Hearth

If Europe had a symbol it would be a well
so that when the bucket went down
it would dredge up a star
its silence deep as the star's displacement
and a simple stellar light
reveal a world of black and white
where things are purified
in a great consolidated inner sea

but the origin of Europe is a hearth
because lightning was directed
to blast the fireplace with soot and ashes
and those who let the bucket down
stood virtuous in their violence
and the water is sheeted over
made bitter by the star
that was worm and not deliverance

A Boy in Dresden

for Christian Schütze, on his 75th birthday

The night of the flak-flowers
when Dresden piled down to the water-meadows of the Elbe
Noah's allegory of the species broke its bars
and teemed, pell-mell, down Tiergartenstrasse –
superlatives on the rampage.
None of them is listed in the book of doom.

Where were you, boy, when hoofs winced on asphalt
and the zoo near the slaughterhouse ring
ran redder round the glare?
You'd gone to school, in a boy's battalion,
sour-cherry stains on your hands
and Virgil's warning to city-builders in your satchel.

In the telegraph room, listening to the static
from the receding edges of the Thousand Year Reich
you recalled the menagerie catching fire
in one of Goethe's later writings:
a chorus of gryphons, lamias, pulcinellas, cranes and empusae;
horror you could quote, less hoof than claw.

From A to B and Back Again

1. Routes (Fernando Pessoa)

Hit the road! Change country!
Always being someone else –
The soul is rootless,
Insisting on the window seat.

Don't belong, not even to me!
Flee in advance, aspire
To the lack of any real ending
Or arriving at the hoped-for.

Now that's what I call travelling!
It also means no luggage
Except my dream of passage.
The rest is land and sky.

2. Travels (Gottfried Benn)

Do you think Zurich, for instance,
is a 'profounder' city,
a place of miracles and incense
and journalistic piety?

Or do you imagine Havana,
white and hibiscus red,
can summon down eternal manna –
fresh wilderness bread!

At Grand Central Station, *dans la rue*,
walking the Lido or Penny Lane,
even on Fifth Avenue,
emptiness guts you again.

Why travel at all? Only late
do you begin to see
why one stays put: to cultivate
the self-sufficient me.

The Decision

Today the council deliberates citizenship,
sitting at curvilinear tables with the usual major alibis:
Koenigsberg, mount Paradise, historical necessity –
GREAT PAX that pardons us our crimes.
Now twelve apostles dance their endless round
and faces smooth with privilege
look up and out, at a shoal of faces looking in.

Could theirs be Leviathan? A committee assembles
in the cantilevered bulwark of opinion,
and the Just City pimps for transcendental purposes
its glass heart, landlocked version
of the Ship of Fools (the boat we're in).
Here are the coral sea and the green heights of forever,
the facts arrayed like fish, their throats slit.

Clueless

1

Every visit is a story of what you did today and every visit tires you. You leave me no clue to what you think it means. Only this – abandonment. The state we're in.

2

Facts: a professional hairshirt I have to wear, like Flaubert's inverted hedgehog cuticle. Except for that time I entered your mind, old precursor, behind the curtains a view of equal hills.

3

Is this the shape of fortitude? I try to draw your hands into the warming shelter of my own. A blatant gesture, and one that shifts accusation to consolation's perfect orders.

4

I'm your man – always at a loss, if not for annealing words. Which must be a clue to what you thought unanswerable, seeing how callously you've abandoned it.

Arrow, Bowstring, Hand and Eye

homage to Aleksander Wat

The hand bending the bowstring
   bends it against its will,

though bowstring pleads its case
   conjointly with the hand.

When hardness climbs the air –
   a subtle fact of feather –

the arrow is the bowstring's loss,
   a recollection of the hand.

Heart-target. It calls the bowstring
   'intelligence made prayer'.

Now target instructs the arrow:
   'Be true.' 'Love me.'

*

The eye. An instance of the heart
   knowing what the hand

does. Arrow, string, hand, eye
   of the sad unicorn –

unicorn who is purest Zeno
   in the art of self-reproach.

*

The heart is a bag of wants.
   Nail it, Nemesis, nail it

with the bright archaic turmoil
   of your flowering arrow:

the one strung by every psalmist
   astride a centaur's back.

1909 Photograph of a Broken Hill Miner

He's standing in front of you, pipe in his mouth
and tallow-stub in his hand as he steps out
blinking into the light, see? Because he can't, at least
not yet, his hands still intimate
with the dark illegible load of a mountain more.
The light maintains its usual flat intensity.
Where he lives is a straggle of humpies, kerosene-tin flues
and roofs lashed down against the elements;
behind him in the seething air
a bare solitary track and the tailings' spill
of the British Mine. A second
sun is making offerings to the god of lead and zinc,
a tarry sediment that seeps from his ears
and stains the pillow. He wants home
before too long and hot, and you're holding him back,
staring at his battered flannel jacket.
Next to him is a stack of trimmings for the stove
and another candle. He mutters,
pipe in mouth, holding his dignity, mutters
like the ore before she gives and makes men ghosts.
Don't think he's speaking to you as a victim
of capital's short way with labour
even though he's stubbled in the dirt that made you rich.
No, he's not speaking at all, and when he does
you won't deny he had it sweated out of him, that black sea
surging across the pillow where he has his head.

Chanson

On the one side the Vosges,
lip of the Paris basin;
on the other the cosy spa towns,
 the Black Forest's deep
 exhalations of the German night.

I stood in someone's shoes, marvelling
at the valley lost to time;
at ideal cities and phalansteries;
 at the glacial frontier lines
 of the Treaty of Utrecht.

There, once, my dream of Europe
lived, a lilac weather
at the very thought of things.
 Reason why the table rose
 and stole away my hat.

Also my belief in word, tact,
humour and the road.
Especially my head sank traceless
 crowing a rusty song
 on the heap at Fouilly-les-Oies.

Proverbs and Maxims from the Hive

1

Persephone's bees –
or just a creed of isms?

2

Imagine a honey-dripper
in the digital hive
whose contagious panic
doesn't stop at doors.

3

Don't ring the bees
or they'll be ringing you!

4

Their idea of time
is silence strained through
the eye of a needle.
(Bee-keeper's badinage.)

5

Come, my Maenads,
to cornflowers and lavender.

6

Two or three chitin
undercarriages putter out
of the universal library's
perfect polyhedron.

7

Sugar's what they make –
salt what they dream of.

8

Gold Napoleonic bursars
on a bed of damask:
old geometric markings
of Péguy's platonic France.

9

Blow, and their casings
rustle like abandoned thoughts.

10

Question for the phalanxes –
what happens to a civilisation
built on the sole creed
of Mandeville's apian vice?

Baudelaire: The Cracked Bell

On winter nights it's bittersweet
to sit feet up by the stove, the gas spitting,
and hear, fog-bound in the street,
its dull throb. How slow a thought is, surfacing...

Bless the rugged throat of that bell!
Still, after all these years, as penny-bright
and regular, dome-hatted sentinel
tolling religiously the watches of the night.

My heart is cracked. Struck by unease
it tries to make the night air hum with music.
What happens then? Its clapped pleas

gag like a blown-away soldier's, clay-thick
in a pool of blood, under stacked dead –
rictus: a colossal straining in lead.

The Unreached

I can still see him, the emperor of atolls, King Taufa'ahau Tupou IV
about to take his yearly flight from Tongatapu
to the port of refuge at Vava'u;
the king and his umbrella, the king and his retinue
of advisors, emissaries, cabinet ministers and umbrella holder...
Clambering back on to my lap, my son resumes
his prolonged study of Little Hans,
a German Australian who has just rediscovered his mother
after untold years of peregrination.
Underneath us, Tonga is so many islands, reefs and lagoons...
In the same plane a commercial vanilla grower,
so corpulent he sits beneath his Majesty on one side
counterbalancing
the six of us on the other (it is a small plane),
practises civility on my wife.
Ears popping, I keep a look-out for the Ha'apai volcanoes,
vents of the trench
deeper than the Himalayas are tall,
where the Australian plate eats the Pacific
at ten centimetres a year...

A week later, the Lord's Day brings rain from the Cloudrider
and we are learning to subsist on taro, manioc, yams,
buckets of red snappers from the coral reefs –
the only fish that still shows hurt.
Ostentatiously we avoid that dread delicacy, corned beef,
ranged in 57 varieties in the local store
with its peeling weatherboard
and planetary bass-note spilling out onto the street –
corned beef, that grows in cans in papalangi-land.
I am brought to know many things, not least by fishermen
who smell of tobacco and flying fox:
the two-hundred year old gifted tortoise from Captain Cook
that remembered to die only in the 1960s;
the fabulous incubator bird
found uniquely on the crater lakes of Niuafo'ou
whose eggs hatch out, feathered, from their steam-vent burrows;
typhoons, lava, and the first day of the world.
Those, and other fully-fledged stories –
Tonga itself created by Tongaloa, whose whalebone fishhook
got stuck in the sinkhole called Deep Thought.

All it takes to be a friendly islander is to cherish the island names:
Fofoa, Nuapapu, 'A'a, Mu'unu, Kapa...
to call in on Tongans in their soft and hairy houses
while the atoll emperor's at prayer
and the Tongan pig (genus: street-urchin) squirms on hot coals;
to admire the carnal red of Neiafu's hibiscuses
petulant on the skin
when the rain comes down and blows them crazy.
But I don't expect someone to ask: what's the *real* difference
between the Latter Day Saints
and the LMS? What's a Mission to the Unreached?
If I knew once, I've forgotten now,
since the body-song of the deeply inset navel
takes us all *toto vaca*
back to the primal tree at the Cabaret Voltaire –
the Pacific islands spread out
like clipped toenails in a great blue bath of Wesleyans
where news still reaches me
of an isolato family caught on the Minerva Reef's high tide,
water to stand on and nothing else around.

Travels with a Donkey to the Bridge of Europe

Deserted esplanade swept by Boreas,
cathedral spire with its cardinal's hat of scaffolding,
tiles ripped off and Latin trees knocked down
that formed a palisade to German forest,
guard to the counterscarps and bastions of Europe,
the solid vegetable peace of post-war.
No place for the ass of Arcady...

                             Perhaps not,
but it's coming, with the soft patience of all donkeys,
out of that prayer on the road to paradise
(now a tourist subtract of eternity),
from a Cevennes of deserted whitewashed churches –
Modestine sold for a burton in St Jean-du-Gard –
to the concrete bridge across the Rhine.
Admire it standing beside me steaming in the rain
getting what it expects: its just deserts,
the wrong use of the rope. Lord Hamlet's quagga,
Fourier's zebra-minus-stripes, Buridan's ass –
it's a writing mule, obedient and still;
upon its uncomplaining back the burden of my thoughts,
a ribambelle of nostrums for the saddlesore.

You can watch it cross the Rhine, a stable smell
among the traffic returning to what the traffic thinks is home,
a donkey with the sphinx strapped to its back
and round its neck as many pots and pans.
O vernacular of all our civilised misapprehensions!
O horse translated into double-Dutch!
Let me be your Sancho Panza!

The Weight of a Day

Jules Supervielle

Solitude, into my room you come, impersonating a crowd:
rain on one man's coat, another dumped on by snow, yet another
burnished by the July sun.
They come crawling out of the woodwork. 'Listen to me, listen to me!'
Each wants to tell me a little bit more than the one before.
This one's searching for a long-lost brother, that one a mistress or a child.
'I'm sorry, I can't do anything for you at all.'
– Not that that stops them launching into interminable digressions:
'Just hear me out, I'll be gone as soon as I've had my say.'
(Their body language means: sit down so we can talk for even longer.)
'But I've told you I can't do anything for you –
hallucinations of the retina and middle ear!'
There's a stranger who begs forgiveness and vanishes before I find out
what he did,
a young woman who's trudged through woods and no native woods;
and the old dear asking my advice: 'Advice about what?'
But she won't say another word, leaves in a huff.

There's nothing now in my room except my desk piled high with books.
Lamplight falls on a head, and a man's hands,
and my lips begin to dream on their own like orphans.

Hope, Art and Labour

1

You'll have to brave the elements, vagrant, go down Argent Street again
and pin the Declaration of the Citizen's Duties to the city hall,
let the gum-trees shed their pods into the Roaring Forties, the whale
                                                        inflate itself
from Ayers Rock's red umbilicus, a special kind of contrivance
for inflating the id and leaving a continent weightless, ballast-free.
Then fly the heft of it, the manila colour of a landmass
bursting with isotopes, that whole citric acid civilisation of juggernauts,
advertising floaters and vast mineralogical undertakings.
Thus hitching the problem of who you are to where you're going,
though you're here to work, to galvanise dead pioneers.

2

Night lights up with stars, cold and crystalline, and the southern cross;
clarity in the world of things – it looks like a substitute for poetry
but isn't, is its occasion, though the seeping desert salt is killing arable land.
Land means abandoned. It aims for the wafer words of inner drought:
infecund, sere, drained, leached, sucked dry, barren, issueless, jejune –
though you're miles away studying animal form, animals never seen before
like the visiting desert dragon, a creature from a Fellini film
that goes for weeks without water, and travels incognito till it lands up
inside a naked garden, its landscape on its back. Also: sonny boy's first
                                                        words,
Habbukuk it sounds like, a messenger between millennial zones.

Pepper trees and bottlebrush flowers are probably obscuring your tracks
but if you look you'll find an aggrieved exile in one of the watering holes
to remind you of your place, how clusters of tolerance work
out of poverty and hardship, and incredibly hard drinking aliases,
people on the point of abandoning their names in a Salvation Army
shelter.
What is the comfort of strangers? It is being left to your own devices
in a town where you can plant baroque cacti to the city life you've fled.
Australia of the open-air treatment. I'm watching people change
from one state to the next, but not their expressions, seeing how things
erode
miles from sea or ship's furniture, here amidst the chemical flats.

4

You're still bursting with love of it, and experience, still believing in hard
work;
a decade gone, a memo addressed to the wife guiding you
across the city of the terror mines, scarlatina, cisterns with a sediment of
lead;
the new police chief standing in the corner without his conversation hat
(not having needed one before), and beside him the god Hermes
sunstruck by the glare, an entire scrub-town, and the helix of your ears
straining for the sound of Bartley's Barrier Brass Band rounding the corner;
Hope encouraging Art and Labour, under the influence of Peace.
What you get is Mario the circus barker drawing ribbons out of his mouth
as he walks across a baked turf of oysters shells and flint chips.

Years after still dreaming of the lemon tree and bougainvillea
in the neighbour's garden in Broken Hill, not dreaming so much as
                                                            smelling
its singeing bush-breath, the same pungent scent of oil and alcohol
added to the flames of shaving by a Maltese, the town's sufferer of bad
                                                            jokes,
his barber's E-number volatile above a dark green curtain of citrus leaves.
My field of vision takes it in, and the ways of bush baroque:
crankshafts in mining country, the ooze of time, salt mica, base materials.
Come and meet him then, ten years younger, a maverick setting out
with hope and high head, not yet a returnee, but already sure that looking
                                                            back
the traveller sees as horizon what is, in fact, his aggregate.

A Nest of Boxes for the Opening of the Scottish Parliament

A box, but not a mahogany covenanters' four-square:
one you might have put your milk teeth in,
tender buttons, stamps, nail-parings, a solar cell
and other incunabula of the life project. Also –

       finder's keepers,
       misbelief but no faith like this,
       latifundian gorse,
       sloes on the Galloway coast,
       the pure spirit with sloes in it a year later,
       earth from Theodosia,
       memories of the Sabbath,
       wee bit sangs,
       cold unboiled peat-water in a can,
       the sleeper's shape,
       another Stevenson lighthouse,
       the-Place-for-Hauling-up-Boats (one word),
       stripped willows,
       the owl on your shoulder,
       calling the saithe, in thirty variants,
       silence's oxides,
       mining by the light of incandescent fish-heads,
       planking the evidence,
       West Nile Street,
       Bundleman and the Justified Sinner,
       adjournment and dispersal,
       knocking your pan in,
       sine die,
       the quiet before the opening of the seals.

First lay its meaning out flat. Then run your finger
over it, from one horizon to the next,
opening and closing, opening and closing it,
as if you were conceding that famous northern threnody
for squeeze-box and bag of guts –

       a life-line,
       a horse's skull,
       a foetus with its thumb in mouth,
       a knot,

a Viking longship,
a crannog,
a minister's falsers,
a day like any day,
a himberry,
a stone skimmed across water,
a bullet,
an egg-bed,
a rare walnut,
a whorlbane,
a washed-up tyre,
a garnet,
a cutty sark,
a queeny,
a fluky goal,
a dwam,
a poor-box shilling,
a shot star,
a stug of burning bush,
a fit-ba,
a V of migrating geese,
a lily-loch,
a dagger over words of the Older Scottish Tongue,
a grannie's hankie.

This is where memory begins
and things are trained to sound themselves,
though you mustn't listen too hard to the noise of time
in that emptiest of escapologists' boxes
or you won't hear a damn thing –

totemism,
box-wallahs of the continent,
the Streamers,
miles and miles of not a lot,
Molucca beans cast up on the Western Isles,
the zaum of the wind in barbed wire,
Ossian read the bans,
the *escueto* style,
the deil as hero and comedian,
untamed words,
Europe's outerling nation,
the aorist imperative of the verb *scholazein*,

hochmagandy,
albino strawberries,
at the gates of the British Linen Bank,
an ear to the ground,
key words,
ease in its skin,
problems from Ibsen that swam across,
imported eau de Werther,
helleborine,
a hand cupped to an ear,
brave faces,
the Thane of Cawdor,
the odd sight of words becoming history,
spilt ink,
the race-tide on Luce Bay,
dates in the Hebrides,
charms,
post offices doubling as grocers,
bog asphodel;

not forgetting how many box-owners, exhausted by time,
walked up their spines to find another box,
one bolted unalterably home though not by themselves –

Linnaeus on Jacob's Ladder,
a spatter of poppies,
soor plooms,
headed notepaper from the John Knox Institute, Geneva,
the Book of Esther,
Sir Mungo Lockhart of the Lea,
Sandy Traill's lament,
things hidden in plain sight,
Engineers Street,
oatmeal with everything,
Pictish Made Easy,
St Kilda's parliament and the eighteen voices answering in chorus,
umbersorrow,
Edwin Muir in the bone factory,
the Old Firm,
forever under the pigeon,
our figurehead coming through the rye,
sheets of rain,
no more shortbread,

a tax on excessive use of the first person plural,
proceedings of the Scotia Bar,
Beuys on Rannoch Moor,
grey zones,
silence (the terrible surrounder),
friends on the Faroes,
Patagonistics,
the undersea Sargossa off the Hebrides,
redcoats landing in France, again,
milk wort and bog-cotton,
my country doctor's box-coat bellying in the wind,
things as guarantors of belonging,
truly remarkable things,
facts unfurling,
quite unremarkable things.

Not a black box and certainly not Pandora's ironic box
(which wasn't a box anyway, but a jar)
with only hope inside, heavier than air, nor even a pill-box,
but a box of rain-and-lowering-sky picked up now
or later, added to, or taken away from, once or many times,
a box of the already-gone and the still-here –

Little Banff and Mid Whirr,
St Rollox,
The Whirlpool (a croft),
Sgurr Mor,
Rest and Be Thankful, again,
Rottenrow,
The Lynn of Lorn,
Little Float (another croft),
Strontian, driven through,
Brig o' Turk,
The Machars and the Rhins,
Loch Hope,
the ascent of the Law,
Hoy,
Rhum, Eigg and Muck,
two Scalpays,
the descent of Canisp,
Clova,
the Black Isle, in Tintin,
Man, from Lagvag,
Foula seen on a winter's day.

Things need cajoling before they can plead the life project
and enter a box's invitation to the labyrinth –
though things may not be worshipped or amassed except
by beginning curators, their boxes under pillows.

> This, and this, and that as well –
> not a list but a syntax;
> less a chamber for goading the past
> than a parliament of voices, in the words of its opening.

2 July 1999

Ten Years: A Psalm

1   after so many barren years, I can talk again as if the dry matter of fact had broken into spate

2   conjuring up another uxorious pet-name, like Monsieur Teste who liked to call his wife 'oasis'

3   and though the world is older, unconscionably older, than when I was a boy

4   we open several years together and let them stain our lips carmine-red (or is it your favourite fuchsia?)

5   the pomegranate of being together

6   now you read to me in German from the Song of Songs, the only erotic book I know

7   the one my childhood fell asleep to

8   and when the children waken us, asking why the fatherly side of the bed is always in turmoil

9   we know we've eaten from the tree, and eaten each other too

10   after all, my fair and comely one, this is what we have to get used to: the burden of our happiness – and us still wedded to making sense of it.

A Promised Land

To come here, almost Biblical with promise
To touch the other life slain on the altar
To stay awake at night, gazing at the pale horizon
To feel the fallenness of institutions

To level with the grass and still be royal
To mingle among an undetermined proletariat
To rise from the quotidian to the stars
To be the cause, partaking of the occasion

To linger in immense Miltonic dark
To avoid the novel ways of resentment
To be witty, saying farewell
To be fond with German words

To tremble on the edge of learning
To make peace with my own scant trade
To know knowledge eats even Eve
To endure the irony knowing it can't be Uganda

Angelology

Desolation angel, restore me to my senses
And the languid manners of insouciance

Be the bright spark that rides connections
Every damn good fall and tumble

Be the intelligent prayer not answered
Pitching me expertly in this hell of circumstance

Be the rivet of my sojourn in reality
Not the thief of hope with his wide addresses

Be the quiddity in a room full of nouns
Surprised by the childhood begging refutal

Be the subtle body of the accident
Ockham's razor to the country past your shoulder

Be my sponsor in the swim of time
Go with me where Calvin never dared legislate

Keep me discomposed with how I live
But let your desolation be other than abomination

Since you yourself are the cost of unguardedness
Polychrome distemper of a Muzot escapee

A recent purpling of bad conscience
Or my disbelief about this deep blue worldliness

Transparency: An Address

Civil society, must we visit you the hard way?

Our diplomatic baggage gets lost in transit.
We don't read much now except on the qui vive.
Our expense account is blue and zinc
and pays for a room with a view
in the capital city no one has ever located –
a midnight afterthought between Paris and Ulm,
a building made of contempt and dismay,
a million unread copies of the DNA.
Here is the philosophy of glass we so admire...

But what will you do when we put down Hegel
and our suits stop thrashing on the rack outside
and the mirror looks blankly at the clouds
and we're not too sure what it means to say
between upset faces and empty places,
the private despair and the public indignation,
Willkommen in Europa, bienvenue à bord...

A Sport of Small Accidents

Once pristine hope
corrodes among the zodiacs
of European Gothic
tamed, sanitised and indignant
all along the glazed
canal-paths and ultramarines
of former ocean floor
the cathedral's thunderbird
impaling the watery city
that sent Gutenberg away
with a flea in his ear
every turn of the wheel
bespoke, motiveless
and locked in contemplation
of one of Dr Slop's
handy obstetrical devices
there is no safer place
insists a teasing easterly
and mind you don't fall off
your latest hobby-horse
though you won't if you move
on ignoring the usual
rhetoric of expectation
and Mr Shandy's motto
routes, not roots

How Long is a Piece of String?

These are the people
who broke his heart, that cat's cradle
of railway connections
from Gare de l'Est to Sakhalin,
string on subset of string
till the circumstances looked infinite.

It was only one cradle
but had many strings and someone
at the end of each.
(Other lives have strings too
and indisputably other
strings have been broken before.)

When his broke it gave way
audibly, like Chekhov's noise-off.
As much the comic rupture
of Plato's midwife's apron-straps
as the acute pianowire snap
of a consciousness.

Trümmerfrauen, 1945

There were no cities,
only elements like fire and water
and in the rubble, dazed,
were men
            and the others
who no longer believed in man
took helmets as buckets
and filled them with stones
redolent of yeast.

Hiding in the River to Escape the Rain

Does the rain suffer of being wet? Who knows.
It's not a thought I'd entertained before you asked.
Why should it? Rain is wet, and it rains
where it wants to, indifferent to the rained on.

It's true. Nobody forced me to bring my dears
to this formal splendid house of inner precipitation.
(Though now the visible sign of my dejection
is flapping in the wind I'm not in a mind to move.)

It was a cognitive error, thinking rain my element.
I've opportunity to accuse myself, to be Job
feeling what it means to come down in the world –
never having thought rain suffered, being wet.

At least the washing hanging in the yard is mine.
Soon I'll have to take it in and strangle it.

The Very Sound of Where We Are

in memoriam Iain Crichton Smith

Could I think you a stranger ever
though you're cold and in the ground, under
a hard bed of obligations? Over
and over I'm being told what I'd rather
not. Of the arctic weather
gone from your face, uncanny northern brother.
Of time, that has no reason to remember.

I wanted to walk you through October
so its gravel psalms might err,
not erring yours. To tread an island river
to the *Mandelbaum*. Slyly to wager
at its source a bud of water
hollows out an ear. Will we never enter
the New Jerusalem? No preacher

says it softly. I don't say either.

A Distance from the Sea

for my parents, in Angus

> Water of Saughs
> Cairn Trench
> Cairn Lick
> Burn of Damff
> Tom Titlach
> Black Shank
> Ewegreen
> The Goet
> Craigs of [...]
> Fleurs
> Gowed Hole
> Wolf Hill
> The Snub
> Gallow Hillock
> White Bents
> Bassies
> Sheck of Inks
> Tod Cairn
> Driesh
> Lick
> The Rives
> Hole of Weems
> Ca Whims
> The Lunkard
> Sneck of the Call
> Black Rigging
> Bawhelps
> Knapps of Fee
> The Ought

Thomas as Imagined by Caravaggio

Nux

Suddenly he caught the white velocity of the tree,
the sanguinary marks, the two thieves
criticising the lack of tact
that nailed them, hands and feet, to make a point.

Crux

Does he always have to revisit the atrocious act,
boyhood's empirical grub thought
balking at the sight of God –
abandoned, wooden, splayed above the world?

Lux

Yes he does, because that's where velocity drives him –
Thomas as imagined by Caravaggio,
a sceptical provincial doctor inserting his index finger
deep into the aftermath
of what it means to need 'the body's evidence'
and live in superstition of the fact.

Joseph Beuys

In one of the striped blue baptistries of Bavaria
self-mythology's pioneer artist is breaking up

though he's left his mind on video –
a Spartan myth to the bee's hum of knowledge.

You can buy it, can't you? The entire bazaar
of blood, excrement, hair, syringes,

gauze, dynamos, gelatine, Leyden jars, vinegar
and used paper. Not that everything's entirely

as he left it: his felted lump of tallow
(that preserved something like human warmth,

material for living, surplus calories
to nourish the mind in its last Russian winter

of machine-age icons and bullet chorales)
is even now hurtling down – a press of flesh,

autobiography and intimate wilderness
borne into the weather-unlike.

All the Old Dears

It's easy to mistake them
for something else, extending
pity into winter light,
the threat of iron beckoning.

The old incline to apathy.
Count them in, the way I'm doing,
the old who lose their sorrows
sipping supper through a reed.

Your castaways, Sisters of Mercy,
left in rooms with the windows
sealed against the weather,
and the gas man for company.

Two or three watch the idiot box
in the departure lounge,
a urine-haunted puce-coloured
room of enforced good cheer –

watch the others chewing the gristle
of something Maisie said;
lips slack, and the gnat of a smile
on the Cenozoic ice sheet.

Millennia tide across the shag
and leave a knot of bladderwrack.
Man is a helper to man,
but love is gone and won't be back.

By Further Knowing

In the early days
Word was a powerful thing.
It might come alive as you spoke it
and was its own enchantment.

Now it goes shadowless
in the great chain of command,
hungry for whatever it is
it can't get enough of.

And you don't know
what Word is.
You love it like the angel of obliquity
you hear so much of.

Word learns to hide
beneath the skin of the material world.
Word is a child,
like you, of surplus.

So why should it bother
to put a body on
inside the lengthening light
of yours – that landscape of brute fact?

It cannot be a mouth at all
except it live
your weaknesses:
immoderate pure ideas, and leached of fact.

Now, when it emerges
from its other shape, consensus,
each gravid cyst
unloads its brusque apostles;

and in our surface world
Word is the most explicit consciousness.
And you don't know
what Word is.

Movement

after Rimbaud

The tug and drag on the banks of the watercourse,
the swallowholes pirouetting at the stern,
the gangway sliding home,
the vast thrust of the undertow
haul through a string of gnostic lights
and serotonin novelties
voyagers – to a fjord pocked with waterspouts
and the sliding mirrors of the Gulf.

Conquerors of the world –
off they go in search of their personal smack trail,
Nikes and the Lonely Planet come too;
men with expert knowledge
of germlines, breeds and classes; on this good ship
repose and vertigo
and the light pouring in
and the terrible nights of study.

Out of the talk among the equipment, blood, flowers, fire, jewels,
the frantic accounting on this *Marie Celeste*,
you can see – rolling like a dyke beyond the pile-driven road,
monstrous, lit for the rest of time – their glaciologies;
all of them mad for C-major statements
and tales of derring-do.

Under the streamers of the upper atmosphere
a couple sneaks off to the bridge
– is it this primitive up-yours people forgive? –
and hum a song. Keep vigil.

Painting with Razors

On Luce Bay my son used to salvage razor fish.
He stored them in his red plastic bucket
until the smell required me to throw them back again.
Never once did he see me shaving with them.

Who's to tell him (though perhaps he knew then)
the living part was eaten by the sea
before the shell became a tool for applying
Scottish Expressionism's thick blue impasto.

In fact, after several months in the brine
those blades were so fragile only his infant hand
could assuage their tentative black
arguments for my loss of northern charisma.

Two Poems on Classical Themes

1. Apollo and the Plague at Thebes

Only a god can save us now,
the god of pestilence
who is also the god of healing.

(And still we build like bees
inside our pulpy isms
the empty house of Being.)

He is there though, Apollo –
standing outside the city
with his caduceus and its snake,

defiantly bearing the question
to our living level eye
that won't suffer what we are –

knowing health is upon us
and no worse contagion.

2. Odysseus Can't Find his Ithaca

Even he must recognise it, the Iliad
stunned by his novel heresy,
the Aegean's seductive overture
to the voyage of the self.

How can tenderness be a help
if knowledge is the place he wants to go?
(Many get lost in the maelstrom.)
Nothing is what he thought it was:

error, if not downright terror
to grasp the basic salesman's trick
of recursive verbal logic
for the janitor at the end of the mind.

Identity was what Odysseus cast off
when he saved his skin.

Frail Craft

Kahn, der klein und schwach...

When you went down
in the cold water of economic reality
a huge heaving sea
knocked you unconscious.

Your world went under too
and all the fond delusions nurtured
since your Biblical boyhood.
What to do? – Jettison

that siren trinity: self-pity,
resentment and special pleading,
whale-days of psalmody
and the Saviour in the rigging;

and remember how you pitched it
(blank butterfly concern)
on Robinson's island:
the little ark among the flags

and you, there, clinging to the rock
on which you foundered.

Strange Weather

Ensemble Convivencia playing Brant's Ship of Fools *in the Parc de Pourtalès,*
Strasburg, July 1999

I saw it in the park –
Europe as a Ship of Fools.

A figure stood upon the prow
and said: 'Behold your mischief.'

Fierce storms of wrong
and rancour were about to fall.

Black clouds would inspissate
and cast us wailing off.

Glib waters were about us:
the royal way was maritime.

O how the ship of Europe rode
the gathering of the nations!

Stiff waves stood in a heap.
The boat was rigged.

Bottler Names

I read Australia's names as trail marks from the Pilgrim.
Now I don't know if I found or invented them,
or if it matters much at all: Mount Fortitude,
Desolation Lake, Murray's Backbone, Strzelecki Creek –
concepts, like everything else in the streetless waste
beyond the Great Dividing Range called *bush*;

bottler names, odd signs of life from those who did
or died where they didn't, marks of character
holding fast to anything upright in the Big Empty –
enormous contagion of what's either 'worked on'
or 'put up with', in fellowship and loneliness;
names of custom and common experience, old-style
as endeavour itself, whose motto ousts Jerome's:
the world is already full and no longer holds us.

The Guest

after Brecht

It was kind to invite him as your guest;
odd, though, to make him feel abject.
Now he ventures to object
in these uncertain terms. 'I protest –

wasn't there *some* way to have been your invitee?
Even a dosser slips his mate some bread!
I wasn't angling for a house or bed,
just a bivouac beneath your chestnut tree.

Words never came, nor the face to take me in.
Cold-shouldered, I felt compelled to go.
Being here seemed a failure of taste,

and so I lost the nerve to be your kin.
Now my wish is seen for what it is: slow-
witted author of such unseemly haste.'

The Large Triumphal Chorus of Medicine

a tribute to Roy Porter

On that chariot commandeered by the Liberal Arts
Reason yokes the horses of the senses
And Prudence drives them with her flails!
Onwards – Dignity, Honour, Glory –
To the house of Medicine, and with such latitude
As might body out what steers the spirit!

Only This

Only this
                the thought it takes
that pushes at my mind
                not faithfully followed
nor properly annealed
                from too much hunger
too much weariness
                of what it might have meant
to rise from a heap
                of lives and numbers
no dreams like Joseph's
                just cruel and blind
numb in the dark
                unbandaged hope

considering the judgement
                and the God who makes it
severest mercy
                discovered more fully
in the thought it takes
                to fill a life
stripped by the wind
                in a storm of laughter
shut out of knowledge
                just hanging around
wondering in the dark
                of the needful life
which might have been
                even true

Family Virtues

Dad was comic postcards
when he wasn't Cotton Mather.
Mum was a regiment
admonishing John Knox.

Son one sniffed Pascal's wager.
Son two lit lucifers.
Son three was a solid rock.
Daughter, only, spoke in tongues.

All of them Brethren.
Exclusive, and proud of it.

An Informant to Alexander Carmichael

'First I'll smoor the hearth
and the militant angels will move over us
like the weather. Then I'll sing a charm
to shield us against everything ruinous
when we go down to sleep,
(you in your bed, I in mine) –

a healing song about the apple tree
and a stoup of mountain water
and rejoicing at the return of the prodigal
who has worn out his shoes,
worn them out, I promise you,
for a season's grafting in the vineyard.'

Baudelaire: Collecting my Thoughts

Be a good child, Sorrow – lie still.
Evening is what you asked for; evening is here.
What does the dark do? It treats a city like a landfill:
relief for some, for others fear.

Sorrow, people are so servile:
they kiss Pleasure's whipping stick as randily
as it can punish them. Each vile
amusement increases shame. Give me your hand,

let's go elsewhere. Look at the Years, long dead
aunties leaning down in their pinafores,
Regret surging from an ice-box of metaphors.

The Sun dosses down beneath a railway arch.
Then, with her Hermès scarf snagged on the marches,
Night. – Listen, child, listen to her tread.

Gutenberg Wings

Item: Strasburg's storks have their wings
clipped so they can fly steadily
(ever more desperately
inwards) to the radiate spokes
of the Brueghel wheels beneath, mist
and the luminous symposia
of cedar trees and Douglas pines,
rooftops polished by the rain,
matrons out in their dressing gowns
and an early morning runner
breathing thick clouds of unknowing;
here and there, vulnerable
landing points in this rinsed morning
of the usual mystery, time
and circumstance and what the mind
might make of history
in one of Europe's scathed idylls;
a pure disconsolate moment
when the dream is freaked awake
by Radio Lyonesse, the talk
of rights and wrongs and the telephonist
on the other side of silence.
For storks are no adventurers,
civil in their life of circuit.
Clipped, so they don't fly back to Egypt.

Alsace is an Island

The border is a fluent one.
Europe swims in it,
leaving effluvia on the chairs
in the Café Brant.

Imagine the war's over.
That soft sound
is what the sea says
shrinking through the eras.

No, it's not. That hubbub
is draft directives
in a language normalised
for EU usage.

And we're the meta-objects
of the administered life;
talkers, chatterers
on the coast of Bohemia.

And this is a waterproof map
to No Man's Land
charted by a common sailor
of the *Neversink*.

King and Queen of the Most Sunken City

just for one day…

Ullmannstrasse. Catch me
dazzled by it:
the Schindler – maximum weight: 12 persons –
and touch the wing of vertigo, the opposite
of those cold objective lessons

brailled by those with a right to history,
psychonauts who put a studded ear
to the panic button, and record the faraway
insinuation –
'Jump, kid, go find a fear.'

I watch a lift clamp on flesh, cuffing
cold shoulders, a face gone. Novice stockbrokers –
all night it hoists them up, the coughing
rich, to the rooftop with its bunker

moss. Might it cut them off, and leave them there,
all cargo gone?
Might it never stop,
this cage that climbs and climbs to the end of air:
the arithmetic of nothing caught in a Dopp-

ler warp, just pulsing with the flow?
Not it, their iron rescuer!
Now I see it for what it is,
fixed in my field of vision, the slow
haunting of our ark of panic by Atlantis –

Plato's city-ship that freights its weight between
ideas of happiness, a century
of level lighted floors where the King and Queen
tell how they drowned, and make it pay.

Heavenly City of the Twentieth Century

Then he got up and went into another land,
tables and chairs on his back, wife and children beside him,
every effort the vanguard of his determination
not to minister to his needs, not to sell his birthright
for an opening in the bespoke thoroughfares;
walking through the stones and coming out unharmed
at the feast of thousands where redemption
might be a name to sit down and rejoice with
and the parting also a meeting place.

But the city he found seemed to have followed him
into the echoey labyrinth of his own mind:
a geometry of choice, the crucifixion of a name.
(Being free to choose there could be no knowledge
of having rightly chosen: only grace could grant that.)
What the city wanted was civility, for a city's sake.
The selfsame admonished him: this is no proper place
for neglect and consequent relinquishment –
the way to heaven is paved with experimental amoralism.

Then he wondered at his gluttony for cities;
at the famine plan: renunciation, silence, petrifaction.
Days from the sea, he dreamed of what the sea might bring,
dreamed of what was once lightning in this city
that hadn't flooded in more than a century,
being mortgaged to a siege mentality. Allegorically
it might also be, shimmering on alluvium, God's City –
a tribunal lit by its own lights, flood and debris
of a mind's life, wife and children weeping.

Falling off the Map

for Peter McCarey

On the cwrwgl of lost poets
we'd surely get to meet – *inter alia* –
Sir John the Ross, still outward bound
to the land of Narragonia,

beside him, those scanted exotes
of the Scottish nation:

Quintyne Shaw (non-extant) and Sandy Traill,
the good Sir Hew of Eglintoun,
Maister John Clerk and James Affleck,
douce Roull of Corstorphine –

late experts in narration
and the textual straitenings of the Clyde.

So sail, good ship *Immemory*,
sail for St Andrews, but allow us first to greet
Sir Mungo Lockhart of the Lea!

Life of the Civil Servants

Some of them like double-agents cultivate
a sense for the nod
and hardly perceptible wink.

Some are amorists of the ice shelves,
adulterers of *is* and *ought*.
They climb to slaughter in their dreams.

Others admit it, but not in public.
They know how to cross the threshold
in any of several languages –

those major character actors of our time.

All are sardonic masters of protocol,
the art of making sure syntax
stops the eye seeing what the hand does –

lovers of the people, which can't love itself.

Song: It Makes Me Wrong

Love, love you go your own way
And leave me wrong about this, wrong about that
Wrong about nearly everything
The way of the wind on the injured ground
Brightness unannounced and a blue moon between
Sweet craving salt at the continent's core

And the geese are a gaggle in the fat grass
And the eggs are rich in molybdenum
And the bells pouring down from the glacier's heel
Say German goitres and French livers
Can't be the way of true love
But peace and doldrums and more of the same

Till you wake with a shiver and understand
One or two small lapsing things
Why light suffers and why you can't grasp
Walking and smiling and the politely tugged hat
Or children rehearsing the Inca
And the wise dada owls meaning otherwise

Now love, when you have to go, watch astonished
How a city opens up, its head agape
And time in a lag, rain and more rain falling
Into the marrow and the night-thresher
Where I sit for a while on the edge of my breath
Wrong about this, wrong about that

This

Fernando Pessoa

They say I fake or lie
With the written word. Not a bit.
It's simply that I
Feel with a kind of wit.
Heart doesn't come into it.

All I put up with or embrace –
Hurts and harms, life's only end –
Is like a level space
Hiding the space beyond.
Some enchanted place!

And this is why I write
As if I'd taken flight
From suffering and the real,
Serious about what isn't.
Feel? – Let the reader feel.

A Sceptical Examination of the Body of French Medicine

Maître et cher confrère, I was trying to practise
your con/science and look what happened.
A patient came in and said: Doctor, take another look at

> my swollen head
> my two members for supporting my head
> my black bile
> my gravel urine
> my fidgety names for being ill
> my camouflage of body art
> my Merck manual
> my snug skin
> my unguents for all parts of the tegument
> my oyster and my Q
> my heart in my mouth
> my ribs run aground
> my enormous and delicate liver
> my spleen
> my brazier of unmeaning
> my body which I give over to you, connoisseur of loss
> my grief, on your hands
> my six senses
> my heart harpooned
> my smell, like a page from Huysmans
> my tactless body politic
> my doubt-armour
> my debts, which you can repay to medicine

and I said, No, it's not like that in my practice:
I'm the sceptical rationalist
who leaves well alone what heals alone…

Salt of the Earth

That brackish lingering Solway smell
when the tide went miles out
and left the spiralled
excavations of sandworms. Salt –

it was our tribute, a cone of oxide
on a Mysore merchant's scales;
a supply of domesticity
for the roundhouse of Ledoux's ideal city;

the crust around our outback house
where the groundwater bore the stain
of aboriginal accusation –
residue of an abstraction so pure

it hardens on terraced flats at altitude:
brilliance that strips eyes
and leaves us, like Lot's wife,
smarting in the vanity of our nostalgia.

Two Steps in the Phenomenology of Walking

1778

Deep in the folded valleys
of the blue mountains of Alsace
Jakob Michael Reinhold Lenz
tried to walk on his head.

1887

Farther south, where the Rhine
bends at Basle, Nietzsche's naked
intellect hit the road –
and had to be put on its feet.

Droit de cité

for Patrick Declerck

In a bricked-up doorway halfway up
one of Strasburg's Black Death prospects,
he sleeps
                miles from the shore
of Fischart's burgher city, miles from help,
on the barest island of himself:
floating bed, bin-bag cushions,
his feet wrapped in rags, and then in rugs –
all the custodial fond junk
of Hernando Cortéz on his final raft.

Go on, son, give him an obol –
there's only the tar and oil
to wade across, the various stations
of the pavement debating club,
the exultant knocked-over sound
of the El Dorado glassware of the night before…
All things come to their succession,
even the washed-up.
                  A delinquent
wrack of biography swells and jugulates:

man in search of the absolute
in one more flood town of the Rhine.

Bucket

A bucket stands collecting rain.
Blunt container, it collects
essence of only ocean
above some dun African savannah.
Capsizer of your head
should you try to plumb it.

It irons a puddle; no wider
wetness than its expanding sense:
matter as a meaning
steadily, irreversibly filling
something (say it bucket, say it)
at the bottom of its need.

All night, a lake lies shocked
above a bucket's tegument. Rain
spites its face. This red morning
foliage brightens the rim,
and hope is such a terrible violence
you, rider, hedge your bets.

Strasburgers on the Beach

Melville invents a foreign language that runs beneath English and carries it off: it is the OUTLANDISH or Deterritorialized, the language of the Whale

Gilles Deleuze

All evening, as the sun goes down
on the darkest continent, I brood on whales,
those stately tops of hills
sardonic on the waves. Out of depth,
they form a mountain range
on either side of me, governing by dint
the surfaces of civil light.

Manners; their arbiters.
I watch the huge hinged tongues
awash with brilliant strokes, swinging
down on potato drills, trenches
where a man might shrivel
exultantly – the old tremendous beast
folding history in upon itself!

Strasburgers are on the beach
clapping, as I step inside the bulk
of pedant Behemoth (a continental Hobbes):
cold, and not at all pacific.
It pierces the Great European Plain
while steam rises from its flanks
with a glazed marmoreal roar.

Iron rungs are planted in its side.
The whale is an ancient municipal baths
annexed to the juvenile shouts
of a generation that thinks
a blessing or a curse is all the same –
cavernous Multiplex gizzard
of a mountain moving out to sea.

I can smell it now, circa 1953;
like old tarpaulin, or a damp hotel
whose endless passageways
debouch on heaps of boulder-clay,
the sodden substance called Verdun
and various subsoil residues
not yet referred to as 'the good place'.

Whale has become a contour-map,
the ordnance landscape of the Rhine,
a hump among the hinterland
of hops and vineyards and the high roads
where people saunter summerwards,
their walking limbs restored
in the manner of Jean-Jacques.

All the glamour of the industrial past!
My only wish: to be spat out
in reach of land, or the promise of land,
redemptive in this air of unreality –
as if land could explain
what rolls ashore on coastal shelves
not classified by Mercator.

So tell me, Strasburgers, what can love
mean to the refrigerated,
the ghosts amassing by the gates,
those doctrinal mysteries
in the city-state cut loose to wander
Europe, a sanctified version of the secular
in couched denial of the sea?

Notes

Third-Person Lion: 'lion' was one of the names adopted by the German philosopher C.G. Lichtenberg (1742–99) when he wished to comment on his own, often very singular doings. *Disgruntlements* couples Goethe's *Hypochonder* and Heine's *Weltlauf*; *The Guest* is a reworking of Brecht's poem *Das Vierte Sonnett*. Calvin's architect is the formidable Alexander 'Greek' Thomson, whose Glasgow buildings, in defiance of Pugin's Gothic revival, were dominated by a concept of the divine that surely owed more to old Geneva than ancient Greece. *Diogenes Looking for Humans* is indebted to the seminal distinction made by the German historian of ideas Peter Sloterdijk in his *Critique of Cynical Reason* (1984) between ancient 'zynismus', with its emphasis on autonomy, and modern 'cynicism', the functionally unhappy product of human resources management.

The three Baudelaire poems which appear at various junctures are *L'albatros*, *La cloche fêlée* and *Recueillement*. Odradek in *Cares of a Family Man* is one of Kafka's stranger protagonists. The two poems about travelling in *From A to B and Back Again* are Fernando Pessoa's *'Viajar! Perder píases!'* (1933) and Gottfried Benn's *Reisen* (1950); Pessoa's famous manifesto poem *Isto* is also translated.

The Large Triumphal Chariot of Medicine bears on an allegory of the senses in Alan of Lille's epic poem *Anticlaudianus*. The abbreviation 'LMS' in *The Unreached* stands for the London Missionary Society, a group of great influence in the Friendly Islands in the early Victorian era; I was able to visit Tonga with my wife and son in 1991. 'DNA' in *Transparency: An Address* is a reference to Alsace's regional daily, *les Dernières Nouvelles d'Alsace*. The names in *Falling Off the Map* would be entirely lost to history were it not for their being included in the roll-call of dead poets in William Dunbar's famous *Lament for the Makaris*. The 'maître et cher confrère' addressed in *A Sceptical Examination of the Body of French Medicine* is François Rabelais, medic, jurist, statesman, anti-Calvinist, abstractor of the quintessence and importer of plane trees into France; his great Pantagrueline Chronicle (Second Book, Chapter 30) also produced the bad dream in *A Vision*.

Strasburg is spelt throughout in the manner adopted by Laurence Sterne in *Tristram Shandy*, which cannily reserved a whole book (*Slawkenbergius' Tale* in Book IV) for discussion of the obscure doctrinal matters which have dominated life in Europe's would-be capital for many years: the phrase 'Strasburgers on the beach' is Sterne's, and given Strasburg's distance from the sea can only be a reference to the coastline of the never-never-land sighted in Shakespeare's *The Winter's Tale*.